# NEVER ENOUGH TO STAY, ALWAYS TOO MUCH TO LOVE

POETRY

SHREYA S

Made with ♥ on the Notion Press Platform
www.notionpress.com

For every heart that has ached, healed, and dared to love once more.

# Contents

# Contents

# Contents

# Acknowledgements

This book would not have been possible without the support, encouragement, and love of so many people.

To everyone who played a part in bringing this book to life, Thank you. Your belief in me, in my words, and in this journey means more than I can express.

To my dear friend, who stood by me through every step of this process your unwavering support, late-night conversations, and constant reassurance kept me going. I am endlessly grateful for you.

To my parents, who became my motivation to turn this dream into reality, your love, strength, and faith in me have shaped not only this book but also the person I am today. Thank you for everything.

This book is as much yours as it is mine.

# 1. Hollow Echoes

Here I am, feeling lost and hopeless, all alone—
Again?
So scared, petrified of what's to come,
I cannot take this anymore, I'm numb.
Wanting to run, to escape, to be free,
Yet longing for someone, for home, for me.
When will this end?
When will I feel like myself again?
Why did they give me the pain they could never handle?
Why was I the only subject to their scandals?
When will I stop,
Wait, and breathe?
How can I believe this is where I belong,
When nothing was ever mine all along?
Things are blurry, yet I see—
People have only taken from me.
Shit really scares me because I don't know how to feel safety,
What even is it says the voice inside of me.
Safety of the home?
No not really
Safety far away from everyone?
Yes yes maybe
Safety far away from them all?

Yes, yes, maybe.
People are them, and I can't give anymore,
Why was I so naïve to let them take it all before?
I don't want to belong to anyone anymore,
For there's nothing left of me to restore.
Things spiral, and I can't bear this ache,
The desire to vanish, the longing to break.
Maybe because the child in me no longer exists,
Lost in a world that never let her grow.
What is left to see in this life?
The pain? The pleasure?
I've had it all and I don't want it anymore
Its agonizing effect didn't leave my body and has left it sore.
With all the pain holding in and the pleasure flushing out,
I know I will never crave this with all my soul.

# 2. Timeless Haze

The feeling of morning, or is it the night?
Lost in the hush between dark and light.
A world half-asleep, yet not fully awake,
Drifting in hours that time can't take.
The sun blurs in, the moon fades out,
Yet neither can tell what it's all about.
Is it the start, or is it the end?
Or just a moment that won't transcend?

# 3. The Mind's Game

And my mind, playing tricks again,
Pulling me back to places I've been.
Echoes of voices, whispers so low,
Memories fading, yet refusing to go.
Loneliness lingers, quiet yet strong,
Like a tune that plays all night long.
I reach for something, someone—anyone,
But the game is set, and I've already won.
Won the silence, lost the fight,
Drifting alone in endless night.

# 4. Fading effort

I used to try, I used to care,
Now I just sit and blankly stare.
What's the point of giving my all,
When every step just leads to a fall?
I stopped reaching, I stopped the fight,
But somehow, it still keeps me up at night.
The weight of nothing drags me down,
Yet letting go still makes me drown.
I don't know if I should fight or fade,
If I let go or just be afraid.

# 5. Strom, I hold

A hurricane so strong, I keep inside,
Nowhere to run, nowhere to hide.
It rages on, yet makes no sound,
A quiet chaos, pulling me down.
I wish it would pass, I wish it would fade,
But it's a storm that I have made.

# 6. Unseen Yet Felt

Alone she was even with people,
Books and songs only ever understood her.
Selfless deeds she always did,
Even forgetting her entire existence.
Desperate she wasn't,
Just wanted love more than a lover.
Fancy things she never liked,
Little things matter more than ever.
Quiet and awkward everyone saw her,
Wasn't any of that in front of the mirror?
Her laugh was contagious,
Just as were her tears.

# 7. Alone

So alone I felt today,
Surrounded by many but lonely in a way.
Waiting for someone to rescue me,
Knowing I wasn't the one to save.
Neglecting me and my presence,
Everyone kept walking ahead.
So viciously people left me away,
Even I forgot I exist till this day.
Sad I wasn't but empty I was as if dying but never dead.
Wish someone would understand but no one ever does.
Knowing this now I have made peace with myself,
Don't need anyone anymore as such.

# 8. Illusion she believed

Like a stranger in my own home,
Someone lost and all alone.
Someone who was with their one,
Yet sobbing to the core lonely with a frown.
Thought that someone knew her and really understood her,
But like everything else she believed.
This too was unreal,
It felt so real, soothing and surreal.
But not everything is as it seems,
Even a flower can prick your skin.
No one can heal her,
Not everyone sees her.
Powerful yet delicate,
Thoughtful yet secure.
Death never scared her,
But she bawled at her own vital.

# 9. Her

She wonders who would love her,
How she could ever be someone's one and only lover?
Broken doesn't define her,
Yet something about that word just strikes her
Rainbow seems really bright to her,
Storms feel peaceful.
Her aura is so blissful and nice,
She can make anyone feel better at just a sight.
Lonely she felt, even in company
All she was left with was agony.

# 10. Tired

How long has it been?
A day, week or month I won't know
Lonely, alone empty don't feel like just words anymore
Something I was, something I am
Don't even know what I can do to change anything,
Breathing feels so hard yet it is the simplest of all.
How do I stay still? How do I not care?
When all of it is eating me alive still.
How do you feel at ease? How do you let go?
When all you wanna do is drown in this feeling of sorrow

# 11. You never understand

What I want is something you would never understand,
Because I am as lost as I can get.
It's not that easy for me which you don't understand,
I need your trust to carry me thats the only way I can get through.
Nevertheless, you will always suspect me,
See my mistakes but never my struggles and the pain I go through.
You see me messing up,
but you never see me dying of guilt and trying to get up
You see crying
but you never see me fighting against all the demons in my head
You see me laying around playing games
but you never understand what games my mind plays against me.
You see how bad I am
but you never see what turned me this way.

# 12. Familiar Darkness

**Familiar Darkness**

It's calling me back like it's my home,
It's not—but it's comforting, here all alone.
I know I don't belong here, that's for sure,
But it's hard letting this black hole go.
It hurts my soul to know,
That a place like this was once where I belonged.
It's okay though—
It's not so anymore.

# 13. Confusion

**Confusion**

Feeling lost as if even the sun and moon have decided not to give me sight.
Hope is the only source which has grounded me still,
Cause if it wasn't for it, I just wouldn't exist.
The light is far but definitely not out of reach,
If I try I might just reach.
Running away isn't the deed I want to do,
Reaching my goals is how I intend things to go.
I don't really know where but I have to move,
As staying here isn't an option as of now.
Something in me is just so sure,
And the other parts of me ain't talking to me anymore.

# 14. Stay if you want

I never thought we'd reach this place,
A quiet distance, a slowing pace.
We don't talk like we used to do,
And I keep fearing I'm losing you.
I never meant to make this worse,
Never meant to twist the hurt.
I only wanted to make things right,
To bring us back into the light.
But when you spoke of letting go,
The world went quiet, time sank.
I've felt pain, I've felt despair,
But nothing has ever felt this unfair.
You held my heart with hands so sure,
A love so fragile, yet felt so pure.
I let you in, no guards, no chains,
Still, I'd trust you through the pain.
If staying means you'll fade away,
Then go—I won't ask you to stay.
But if there's warmth still left to find,
Then stay, if our hearts and souls align.
Not for the past, not out of guilt,
Not for the walls we once had built.

Stay if you want to, if love feels true,
Stay—only if you choose me like I choose you.
Here's to me
Here's to loving myself a little more,
To knowing my worth like never before.
I may not fit where others stand,
But that doesn't mean they define who I am.
Here's to embracing all I am inside,
The flaws, the scars—I wear them with pride.
The good, the bad, the lessons I learn,
Every piece of me has its turn.
Here's to a new year, a canvas so wide,
To dreams unshaken, to standing with pride.
Here's to choosing myself each day,
To living, to growing, in my own way.

# 15. Perfect

You are just the perfect person I know.
I don't know how, when, or why, but I think I am in love with you—every atom of your being.
No matter how hard I try to deny it or avoid it, I can't, because it's clear. After a long time,
it is all clear—you are all that matters to me, and it's been a long time since something mattered so much.
You are the beautiful plant I want to take care of, water every day,
talk to in silence when people are away.
I want to help you and help you help yourself.
I don't want to be your therapist, nor just a friend—
anything more, anything else.
I want to be there; I want to lose myself in you.
But now, there is no "me" to begin with,
because all I see around is "us."
Things are making me anxious because I want this to work out,
but then, at the back of my mind, I always think to myself—
is this really what I want?
I guess only time can tell. Until then, my love,
I will write to you every day.
In spite of you having no clue,

I will love you in every single way possible.

# 16. For the First Time

For the first time I know that if I fall, you will catch me,
For the first time falling in love doesn't seem scary.
It excites me and calms me down at the time,
Anyone can give you butterflies in the stomach but only a few can stop the storm in your head.
Many can make you happy but only a few can give you peace,
Everyone can make you laugh but only a few understand the pain behind your smile.
Anyone can offer you a shoulder to lean on but only a few offer a hand to hold onto,
Many can hear you but only a few listen.
Everyone can touch your body only a few touch your heart,
Many can see your body naked but only a few dare to see your bare soul.
Anyone can know things about you but only a few know who you are,
Everyone can involve you but only a few include you.
Many may fall for you but only a few will stay in love,
Anyone will promise to be there for you but only a few are there for you.

# 17. To Be Loved

Oh, to be loved truly, genuinely—
Maybe just for a second.
To be desired with one's entire heart,
To be someone they cannot stop thinking about.
To be the one someone has waited for forever,
Oh, to be perfect in someone's eyes, even after every mistake and every crime you committed.
To be loved for who you are and not the perfect version of you,
To be loved for every perfect and imperfect part of you.
And maybe, just maybe, that second could last forever.

# 18. A Living Masterpiece

Full of sunshine, joy, and glow,
Her smile is so infectious it sets the world in flow.
Pretty, beautiful, and gorgeous she may be,
But that never defines nor limits her destiny.
Strong, bold, and elegant,
Fierce and fiery—her aura is magnificent.
If you get to know her,
Life without her is nothing but misery.
She once said she wanted to be poetry,
Oh, but who will tell her? She is already a living masterpiece.
No poem could ever do justice to her grace,
So let me tell you this, honey—you are someone for whom books are written.

# 19. Teacher

To the one who taught me how to love,
To the one who taught me patience.
To the one who stood by me no matter what happened
To the one who reassurance me still,
Even tho it's been days.
To the one who knows my potential,
And never let it go in vain.
To the one whom I am blessed with for eternity,
Or so I hope, cause losing you would be like losing my soul.

# 20. The Look

**The look**

We don't have to use words to speak,
Our eyes say it all just in a heartbeat.
The way you get everything without me having to say anything
has made me fall for you even harder than I already was falling.
Me walking away from you and you letting me go
was the biggest mistake we ever made.
Not wanting to let go
and willing to hold on has been our biggest strength.
Rough times we both have seen, even when they were not the same, a part of them has always been.
The way you look at me says everything words can't say
and the way I want to look at you says everything I can never accept.

# 21. We Are One

I know now who I am to you,
I know now how you feel.
I see us for what we are,
Not just fate—but something real.
If not you and me, then who?
Without us, what is true?
Oh love, how long will you take to see?
We are not two—we are one. We are we.

# 22. This Moment

Here you are, sitting so close to me,
Oh, how I wish to stop time right here.
But this moment is too beautiful to be intercepted,
So I let it linger, let it stay near.
Look at you, smiling at something so small,
Yet in your laughter, I find my all.
If only you knew what your presence does,
How even silence feels like love to me.

# 23. Him

Safer she felt in his sight,
Knowing she was his only dynamite.
Knew for sure he will be there for her in a beat,
Because he was always hers, to begin with.
Clueless as she was, she knew one thing for sure,
They will be together till the end of the course.
Falling for him every day, even harder than before,
She kept moving forward fighting the whole world.
He was her light and her hope,
Knowing no bounds to the bond they hold.

# 24. Love?

And to be loved by him
I would be the side character in everyone's story
To be in his prayer
I will be the sinner for everyone
To be understood by him
I will be the villain for everyone
To be the one he picks
I will be unlovable to everyone
To be the one he stays with
I will be the survivor no one wants to live
Oh to be his
I will even lose existence

# 25. A Home in You

It felt like I had the whole world today after so long,
It felt like I had something to lose at all.
It felt like I was full of light and beaming it all out,
Like I was the master of stars.
The dictator of the moon and the sun,
Who would literally dance at your thought.
I swear I have never felt like this before,
And the thought of losing this now makes me shiver to the core.
It's so blissful to know you exist,
Such a pleasure to call you my friend.
To be your home is the only dream I have,
Happy, comfy and smiling is all I will ever want you to be.

# 26. Love

Falling in love we call it
But what if it's about rising in love instead?
What if being around that person makes you better
Instead of losing yourself?
What if it's not about being with them all the time
But wanting it anyway?
What if it's not about finding your better half
But finding yourself?
What if it's not what happens at first sight
But something which grows with every sight?
What if it's not about sacrifices
But compromises made for one another?
What if it's not about putting effort into them
But effortlessly putting them first?
What if it is not something we feel
But something we do?
What if it's not a noun
But a verb?
Falling in love we call it
But what if it's about rising in love instead?

# 27. Safety net

Finding the one,
Who never walks away.
The one who feels like home,
Having that one go-to person.
Someone you know you can call anytime,
Someone you know will run to you every time.
Someone you know will always have your back,
Even when you do something stupid or wrong.
Not someone you take for granted,
But someone who is your safety net.
Someone you know will catch you if you fall,
Someone you know you can yell or shout on.
Someone who you can be the most raw version of you,
Someone who can accept, understand and love you through it all.
Finding the one,
who never walks away.

# 28. Illumination

How are you so full of light and glow?
How do you fill others with your warmth,
Yet keep your own pain hidden below?
How do you give away what is yours,
Sacrificing pieces of yourself with such ease?
Where did you learn to let go,
To love without expecting, to suffer in peace?
So stable, so composed,
Yet every word you speak is alive on its own.
How are you everything one could need or want,
Yet always leaving a little less of yourself unknown?
How do you recharge, how do you heal,
When the weight of the world rests on your shoulders?
For all I know, you carry your pain
Alongside a million others.
Do you ever find love when you need it the most?
Is anyone truly yours, even just for the weekend?
After wandering through the darkest forests,
How have you resisted the wickedness the world has to offer?
How did you keep the sanity of your heart and mind intact,
When they were crushed before grown?
How are you, darling? Please be honest now,
For all I am here is to love and to lose myself for your cause.

You don't have to be afraid or bear this alone,
For all that you need, I am ready to become.
You are your own light, you need no one to shine,
But should you ever dim, I will glow for you.
Nothing is brighter than you and your smile,
And that is all I will ever pray for.
Delicate you are not, but sensitive—surely so,
How you've held yourself together remains my greatest wonder.
Oh, my love, you are an ocean of love,
Yet all you've ever received are thorns from the rose.
Today, that shall change, my dear,
For now, a waterfall of roses blooms just for you.
Just take a step ahead, and I will run to you,
But the choice will always be yours to make.
No matter what, I will always be near,
Shining the same light upon you
That you so selflessly share with the world.
For all I know, you deserve more than anyone,
Yet you've been deprived of love for far too long.

# 29. The Little Things

It's not the grand, the loud, the bold,
But in the quiet, love unfolds.
A call just to hear my voice,
A text that brings a moment of rejoice.
Noticing sighs between my words,
Hearing the silence left unheard.
The way you see what I don't show,
The way you stay when others go.
It's in the effort, soft yet true,
The little things that make me choose you.

# 30. My person for sure

Friendship isn't just a word,
It's a promise, felt, not heard.
It's knowing someone will always stay,
Through every storm, come what may.
Someone who sees both scars and grace,
Yet still holds you in a warm embrace.
Who steps beyond their comfort line,
Just to make sure you're doing fine.
They may not always have the cure,
But their presence makes you feel secure.
They'll speak the truth, raw and real,
Yet guard your name with an iron will.
Not just a friend, but so much more,
The one whose love is at your core.
A bond unshaken, tried and true,
My person—is forever, you.

# 31. A place like home

Came here for knowledge, came here for fun,
Took so much more and left a part of me behind.
Don't know how or when we became one,
Felt like a family—no one grew apart.
So many memories, conversations so bright,
Leaving with the urge to hold on tight.
Feels like home now, not just the land,
But the people who held me with open hands.
Not only lessons to savour for life,
But experiences etched in heart and mind.
Hot and humid the climate was,
As our hearts breathed in the warmth of love.

# 32. Forgiveness

Forgive me if possible,
Forgive yourself for being with me.
Let go of the pain and create a promising future,
Which is the only thing that you deserve.
Hurting you, causing you pain was never my intention,
I just wanted to make it all better and I did worse.
It aches my heart to see you in agony,
All I wanted for you was tranquillity.
Helping you heal I stabbed myself,
I should have loved you selflessly but from a distance.
Guarding myself I let you flee,
All I did was supposed to be done otherwise indeed.
Forgive me if possible,
Forgive yourself for being with me.

# 33. The Almost, But Never

Lost in the pool of emotions I don't know what to do,
You feel like my person even when you aren't true.
I wish for you to be the one every day,
Somehow I am proved wrong day after day.
My heart's heavy and torn,
Only your touch can heal the poor thing back to whole.
Why is it so hard to love me for who I am?
Am I not the one you should have chosen by now?
I can't help falling in love with you,
Even if you wanna tear my heart in two.

# 34. Falling Alone

So many things exist within me,
All at once, they catch hold of me, then let me go free.
It's been a while since I realized I love you,
But tell me—how can you unfeel a feeling if it was true?
How can I not care, not search for you everywhere,
When just your presence lingers in the air?
One look, one glance makes my heart flutter,
Not looking at you feels like a missed opportunity I muttered.
To be yours, to be your one, is all I ever craved,
But you never looked at me that way, to begin with.

# 35. Never Enough to Stay, Always Too Much to Love

Why am I invisible to you?
Why am I never enough?
Why am I always left to feel this burning pain,
Like a knife stabbing my heart again and again?
When will this end—after all?
Can I just rest?
Rest in someone's arms, someone who won't leave, no matter what.
Can I be loved once, with all of someone's heart?
Can someone care enough to break down all my walls?
Am I just meant to be a burden,
Nothing more than a passing name?
Will I always be someone they just know of,
But never someone they claim?
Am I the reason everyone left?
Was I not worth fighting for?
Did they just not try hard enough?
Or was I easy to ignore?
Am I really so easy to replace?
Will I never be someone's first choice?

Why am I always the one giving,
Yet never receiving even a little in return?
Why am I so hopeless?
This is the last thing anyone wants.
I say I want to be left alone,
But really, I want someone to be alone with me.
I know that will never happen,
Because people don't really care.
They use you, and when they're done,
They leave—just like they were never there.
It's okay, it's just the way things are,
Why bother… when you'll end up alone after all?

# 36. Maybe Love

It's been forever even so I am still holding on,
To everything we had or I thought we had.
Someone I love and care for,
Someone who loves and cares for me too maybe just not enough.
Not enough to accept me,
Not enough to embrace me, to help me bloom
Someone who feels like the comfort of home after having a long vacation,
Someone who pricks like the truth of the thorn around the rose.
Someone of my own yet somehow unknown,
Someone who feels perfect even when isn't.
Someone I know isn't mine to keep,
But feels so wrong to let go.
Ultimately letting go is the only option,
Not only for my peace but also for his betterment.
As losing me is the only way he will thrive,
And the only way I will learn how to shine through this darkness of sorrow.
I have high hopes for his future,
Even if I am no longer in it.

My heart will always carry him around in a corner of my heart,
Which is only devoted to him where no one else other than him can enter, not even me.
There always be a part of me which will move at the thought of him,
But will never relapse into the oblivious cycle of becoming his

# 37. Lost in Your Absence

I don't feel like myself since you left,
Unknowingly, you became a part of me.
A silent comfort, a presence so familiar,
I never knew I'd feel this empty.
I have searched in words, in faces, in places,
For something I lost but couldn't name.
A quiet ache, a longing so deep,
Like a song I forgot but still hum in my sleep.
And now that I see you once again,
I finally know what I've been missing.
It wasn't just you—it was the way I felt,
The version of me that only you ever held.

# 38. Distraction

Why did you promise to love me and leave me,
Why did you show me so much affection if you had to take it away?
Why was I not enough to make you want to stay,
Why were others so fascinating in a way?
Why did you assure to heal every broken part of me,
When all you were gonna do was run away.
Why act like you genuinely care,
When in reality if you did you wouldn't act this way.
Maybe it wasn't love, care or affection
But yet just another distraction.

# 39. Defeatist

So close yet so away,
How did we get anyway?
How did you never sense the pain,
Which kept growing in my heart every day.
You saw in all on my face,
Yet you never stopped your pace.
Waited for you to say it to my face,
But you overlooked my pain and savoured your dissent.
Now it's been too long,
Despair has become a fragment of my own.

# 40. Stairs

You left me on the stairs,
In the middle with nowhere to go
Frozen and so out of place I felt,
Didn't know how or where to go.
I wanted to reach out in a heartbeat,
cause I knew the taste of peace.
As every movement was paid with the cost of me,
Which choked me every time just a little bit.
Couldn't stay there couldn't run away,
So free yet stuck so profoundly in a way.

# 41. Breaking up

Help me make it clear,
I have started to fear knowing you for ages makes it clear.
I feel you awake after I sleep,
What you do is a mystery indeed.
Knowing I will meet you tomorrow,
Makes me feel sick.
Not showing my emotions is not my treat,
I know you would laugh and say it's just a trick.
I would break down saying "don't do that",
Why me? is still my question but why would I ask?
Knowing you can hide things I have started it too,
Me feeling sick is still your clue.
These days you don't pay much attention to me
Which makes things easier for me.
I have started a new life without you
Where I have my family and friends which are better than you.
Friends are best family is perfect,
I choose you over them was my biggest mistake.
When I want to break down I do it to myself,
Knowing you are not mine now but someone else's.

# 42. Broken Beyond Repair

How are you so happy with her,
When you said you were broken beyond repair?
How does your heart beat so freely now,
When it once carried nothing but despair?
You told me love was just an illusion,
That you had nothing left to give.
You swore you'd never heal from the wreckage,
Yet here you are, learning how to live.
A heart only beating, but never for love,
A body only living because death hasn't touched.
So why does she get to have all of you,
When I was left with the shattered remains?
Why does your laughter sound so real now,
When with me, all you spoke of was pain?
Was I just the storm before the calm,
The weight you shed to finally breathe?
Was I only meant to show you love,
So you could give it all to someone else with ease?

# 43. The Man I Need

I need no gentleman,
No man to fulfil my wishes.
No genie, witch nor a magician,
Just a man who carefully listens.
Not a man who pulls the door or the chair for me,
But a man who knows how to respect and adore me.
Not a man who brings me flowers,
But a man who brings a smile to my face.
Not a man who buys me fancy things,
But a man who gives me all his efforts.
Not a man who is the knight to my princess,
But a man who is the king to my queen.

# 44. The Truth

I wanted to reach out, just to say,
You are loved in every way.
Even when shadows cloud your mind,
The warmth of love is not far behind.
In the moments you feel unseen,
Lost in echoes of what has been,
Know that loneliness tells a lie,
Love still lingers, standing by.
Your past may whisper, cold and untrue,
But it does not define you.
You are cherished, you are light,
Even in your darkest night.

# 45. Respond Don't React

Accepting our emotions helps us avoid problems
Instead of misunderstandings we have peaceful discussions.
Knowing our emotions wholly ourselves,
Helps us and others to know what to do next.
Once we understand taking action isn't hard to do,
The only thing left is to calmly express what we go through.
After this, I hope we all will know,
One should always respond but never react.

# 46. Meant to Be, In Any Way

I remember the moment I realized I had fallen for you—
Always wanting to be near you, finding excuses to stay close,
Attending every lecture just to see you, to sit beside you.
At your sight, my heart would light up each time,
And in your absence, something always felt misaligned.
The feeling never faded—it only deepened with time.
I knew this was something different, something real,
You made your way into my heart and claimed your space.
And though I never say it aloud, I love having you there.
From falling in love to growing in love,
Every moment with you has felt like a blessing.
One thing I know for sure—
You belong with me, whether as a friend or a lover.
Something in me feels like home with you,
Maybe I've just fallen for the friend of my life.

# 47. Unspoken battle

Why do I always have to say I'm not fine,
Why must my pain be spelled out in lines?
Why am I the one who always understands,
Yet no one seems to see what my heart withstands?
Why do I walk away when I need them the most,
Why can't I just be myself, open and close?
Why am I so scared—what am I scared of?
Maybe of losing, maybe of love.

# 48. Timing or Fate?

I am so confused,
Like what?
Why does everyone do things at the same time?
Like a rhythm I never learned, a pattern I can't define.
Rushing forward, all in sync,
While I stand still, too lost to think.
Is it fate or just bad timing?
Or am I the only one still rewinding?

# 49. Overthinking

Tried understanding, yet misunderstood I felt,
Wanting their attention, but none I would ever get.
Pain—oh, the only thing that proves I'm alive,
A silent companion, a reason to survive.
They call me foolish, too fragile, too weak,
As if my thoughts are nothing but storms they won't seek.
Overthinking, they say, just let it all be,
But if they listened, maybe they'd see what is true.

# 50. Naked Truth

Anytime, anywhere whenever I let you in,
You find a way to ruin things and me with it.
You leave me alone which I never minded at first,
But because of your false hope, I feel lost in the way.
Don't get me wrong I ain't afraid to be known,
Rather it's the only I want to own.
I hate this feeling of rejection,
I just cannot handle this dejection.
I don't know if you see this, see me going through so many fractions,
To reach the destination which is exposure to my insides from within.
Even so hard I take a step back in,
Only to lose another battle as I already knew I wouldn't win.

# 51. Iniquity

Trapped yet freed,
Shallow yet deep.
The wound in her heart,
Kept bleeding till it healed
Nor happy nor sad,
Not broken or intact.
Not bright nor gloomy,
Not alone or in company.
Alone yet never lonely,
Content she was even in her misery.
She lived while she died,
Like demise was her way of living.

# 52. Maturity

Realizing that losing everyone other than yourself is okay,
Realizing that people have an expiry date, just like things do.
Realizing that you were born alone and will die alone,
What really matters is how many people you made content and full of joy.
Being detached doesn't mean not caring,
Instead, it means knowing what to care about.
Being a state of you and not letting the surroundings bother that,
As you are all that you are searching for.
Looking outside and longing for more,
Only to find the answers within your core.

# 53. What they don't see

People don't see you trying so hard,
But they see you having fun.
They don't see you helping everyone,
All they see is how close you are to everyone.
No one makes an effort to make you smile,
Even when all you do is smile for others.
How is the world so ignorant of your beauty,
When what you are is so dam pretty.
How are people not staring at you,
Just in hopes of feeling heaven on earth.
How are you around everyone?
Yet in no one's heart?
How is no one's heart aching to be yours?
How is no one willing to woo you to make you theirs?
Is something wrong with the world?
Or is it true that they say only the one who falls in love sees the real beauty of your existence?

# 54. Hope

I know Your Nights are Dark and Light Seems Far
You had Your Own Battles and that's what caused those Scars!
But that doesn't mean that you gave up and keeled
It means that you fought, you survived and you healed!
Remember when it's Dark, stars still shine?
And wounds do Heal, be it Yours Or Mine!
If stars don't burn, who would show the path to the Lost?
They still shine bright, even at their own Cost!
I am sure it will be fine, forever, no pain lasts!
As you have made your way through everything,
Trust me, this too shall pass!

# 55. Drifting

Nor empty, nor sore,
I don't know what it is to be at a peaceful shore.
I kept swimming, that much I know,
Chasing tides that refused to show.
Knowing, not knowing, what lay ahead,
Yet moving forward, by hope I was led.
An endless ocean, a nameless quest,
Maybe the journey is what I know best

# 56. Not crush but something like it

The way you look at me says everything words can't say
And the way I want to look at you says everything I can never accept.
Something in me wants to have you around,
One more glance, one more laugh,
One more step beside you, just one more moment.
To feel your eyes on me once again,
Feeling shy and smiling at you one more time,
Watch you smile back at me with a smirk on your face,
Brushing it off like it doesn't mean anything else.
Beaches and playing in the water like kids will always be our thing,
With the dash of sunset along the line.
Mysterious yet familiar feeling,
Like home but still unknown.
You cherish the child in me,
and adore my mature side as it is known.
Small talk is all we do,
Yet so fulfilling they make us feel like a fortune.

# 57. Nature

Those small drops of water to say goodbye to the clouds to fall down from the top to the bottom just to be one with the ground.

Ah, that's love.

Ever wondered why we love looking at the stars?

Its because it gives us hope that even when there is a lot of darkness around us, a little bit of light [positive perspective] can even make the messy darkness look beautiful.

Ah, that's hope.

Isn't this enough to keep us going? Nature really teaches us everything we will ever need to know.

# 58. Never Again

Wishing to talk but knowing it isn't possible,
Wishing to laugh with you but that isn't happening ever.
Wish to once again feel belonged yet I fail,
How bad it hurts knowing we can never talk again.
We won't ever meet, never did I once thought,
Felt like we were meant to be forever but in the end, it never really lasts.
Feeling sorrow or annoyance won't give me another chance,
Only if I knew how bad it was bound to cast.
I know that this is wretched,
But I see you happy and somehow seem to fulfill with it.

# 59. Fools love

I believed every action,
Even when you said don't.
Trusted in your strength and will,
More than you ever knew or wanted to.
All I gave you were words of admiration,
Whispered softly throughout the day.
Even when alone at night,
You left me to cry and fade away.
I only saw the beauty,
Ignored the shadows in your eyes.
Wanting to show you the best parts,
Hoping you'd recognize them in yourself at times.
Went miles out of my way,
To ease your burden.
Expecting no thanks, no praise,
But even a glance would have felt great, I am certain.
They say you can't make somebody love somebody,
But that's never what I wanted for myself.
All I ever wanted,
Was for you to finally learn how to love yourself.

# 60. The Ones Who Walk Away

So hard, yet so easy, to walk away,
Never knowing what someone thinks of you anyway.
Leaving is the best,
But what if it's your biggest mistake?
You are not even seen when present,
If you go, how would people even know of your existence?
Isn't it good to not be known?
Yes, but what if all you want is to be found by that one person?
What if there is no person for you?
I guess it's okay—what would that person even do?
Maybe you are that person for yourself,
Or maybe you missed that person because you walked away.

# 61. Unspoken Pieces

Bleeding through words, yet voiceless I stay,
A puzzle of echoes, scattered away.
Fragments of thoughts, too heavy to mend,
Stories unfinished, with no way to end.
I write, I carve, I try to be seen,
Yet remain lost in the space in between.
Maybe one day, these pieces will fit,
Till then, I bleed through words—bit by bit.

# 62. Ache of Love

My heart aches, but I'm not torn,
Not shattered, not lost—just strangely worn.
I want to cry, but the tears won't fall,
How can I feel pain when his breath makes me feel alive?
I've known betrayal, pain, and nights too long,
But this, this is different—neither right nor wrong.
Expectations wound, but love stays true,
The only thing that keeps me from breaking is you.

# 63. Chance

I know you like being single, free in your own space,
But there's something I need to say, a question I must place.
I don't know how to convince you, what words to say,
But I hope this is a good start, in a quiet, honest way.
Your heart, so guarded, yet I can see the light,
Maybe, just maybe, together we'd feel right.
I know the risks, the doubts you hold dear,
But I'd like to prove to you, my intentions are clear.
So here I am, asking not for love but just a chance,
To show you that with me, you won't have to dance alone in life's trance.

# 64. Lifetime

You were there when no one else stayed,
A distant warmth that never strayed.
A laugh, a voice, a familiar face,
A home where all my things are placed.
You made me smile when I had no reason,
Turned my darkest days to sun.
When living felt like the hardest choice,
You reminded me to hold on tight.
It made me feel alive, pulled me through,
A reason to live when I had none.
Not just a show, not just a name,
But a lifeline pulling me from pain.
They call me foolish, say it's strange,
To watch, to feel, to love this way.
But they don't know what you have been,
Or how you've helped me find my way.
Maybe you'll never know my name,
But I have known you all along.
And no matter what, I'll always stay,
With you—where I belong.

# 65. All that he is

Kind is who he is, steady and true,
A warmth in the cold, a soft golden view.
Gentle hands, a heart so wide,
A love that stays, never hides.
Handsome, yes—but more than that,
A soul that speaks where words fall short.
Not just handsome, not just wise,
But someone who feels like home in disguise.

# 66. Just for a night

I can feel your eyes on me, and I want to look back too.
Maybe it's nothing, maybe it's everything,
Or maybe, just maybe, I'm falling for you.
The way you laugh feels like a melody,
I laugh, and you tilt your head like it's music.
You are warm, like a quiet sunset,
And I—someone who cannot live without its glow.
So why not let the universe decide?
Let's not name it, not rush it, not hold it too tight,
Just exist in this feeling, just for tonight.

# 67. New

Feeling new today doubt that it will last
Wishing to know tomorrow's like yesterday's pass
Looking for good fortune which should last
Having a spirit indeed which shall not pass
It will be the face to my past
Creating new sunshine to my plants.

# 68. The One Who Listens

How does it feel to be the sweetest? I might ask
I wonder how on point he always was.
Smart, calm and Composed like a therapist,
He listened to my endless rants, day after day.
Never once did he complaint nor will he,
I know for a fact cause that's who he is
Sharing a bit about himself is harder for him than others,
Yet he tries while being nervous.
Alone he used to be but lonely he never was,
He's always loved his own company.

# 69. Cost of Tomorrow

We humans make things so complicated, don't we?
Chasing a future we may never see.
Holding our breath for a day not yet here,
While the present slips quietly, disappears.
Nothing is forever, yet we still delay,
Trading our sunshine for skies that are gray.
It's okay to hope for another sunrise,
But is it worth losing today in disguise?
We dream of tomorrow, we plan and we wait,
Forgetting that time never stops at the gate.
So live for the now, let your heart be free,
For tomorrow is nothing but a maybe.

# Author's Note

To everyone who has loved, lost, and found love again.

This book is for the ones who found pieces of themselves in another,

And for those who had to let go to truly find themselves.

Writing this book was as much about understanding love as it was about understanding myself.

In its pages, I poured my fears, my hopes, and the quiet longing that comes with being human.

Some of these words are fragments of my own heart, while others are echoes of stories I've seen, heard, or felt in the spaces between moments.

May these words remind you that love, in all its forms,

Is never truly lost—it only transforms, lingers, and finds its way back to you.

— Shreya S

www.ingramcontent.com/pod-product-compliance
Lightning Source LLC
La Vergne TN
LVHW041132150826
845673LV00007B/2289